PASTOR BRENDA STEWART

Fit

FOR THE

FIGHT!

THE VIGILANT FIGHT OF FAITH FOR MY HUSBAND, MY FAMILY, AND MYSELF

3

FIT FOR THE FIGHT
The Vigilant Fight of Faith for My Husband, My Family, and Myself
by
Pastor Brenda Stewart

Copyright 2013

Published by Merle Ray, The Noble Groups
www.NobleGroups.com
Printed in the U.S.A.
All rights reserved.

For bookings or orders Contact Pastor Brenda Stewart
www.PastorBrenda.com

Photography by:
Dayna Castelberg
Remember When...Photography
832-643-7500

ISBN: 978-0-9893535-6-4

By
Pastor Brenda Stewart

Table Of Contents

TABLE OF CONTENTS
CONTINUED

DEDICATION

To my husband, Pastor Mitchell B. Stewart, Sr.

Without your transformation, I would not be able to share this message. Thank you for the courage to make a comeback! I praise God for you and the Vision of restoring lives by the grace of God!

FOREWORD

By

Drs. Mario and Regina Villela

In a culture where there is a feast of literary works...there is a greater famine of genuine stories by authentic authors. Authors who have tasted the bitterness of life served without notice or warning. We know this story firsthand. We have observed the author both up close and at a distance. This is a story about a woman who has been relentless in her pursuit of victorious living in the heated battles of life. Pastor Brenda Stewart has been to hell and back. For more than twenty years, demonic forces have attempted to tear her life apart, tempting her to abandon her deep love for God and His purpose for her life. In this deeply candid and vulnerable life story...you will be both inspired and challenged. Inspired to rise above the darkness in which Satan desires to hold you captive and challenged to soar to the heights of victorious living always found above the storm. Fear will lose its grip and the faith that makes all of us *"Fit For The Fight"* will arise!

It is with extreme gratitude that we are writing this foreword for our friend and comrade in the faith, Pastor Brenda Stewart. Fasten your seatbelt and prepare for the high altitudes of a Throne Room experience. We are confident that as you read these pages you will be filled with victory, joy and hope for your life's journey with Jesus!

–Drs. Mario and Regina Villela,
Servants of the Streets Ministries,
Elkhart, Indiana

INTRODUCTION
RUNNING FROM A FIGHT

As Brenda Stewart, I have been a licensed minister of the Gospel since December 10, 1989, Founder of Victorious Women of God Fellowship (a ministry to females) and Pastor of Grace Restoration Church along with my husband, Pastor Mitchell B. Stewart, Sr., Founding Pastor and Director of Freedom Institute for Recovery Management (The FIRM). We are the parents of four adult children, ten grandchildren, and many spiritual children too numerous to count. But it has not always been so. Our calling to serve in ministry was birthed out of our pain, toil, and tears. What you see today is the direct result of the miraculous power of God that delivered my husband in March, 1992 from a crack-cocaine addiction and delivered me and my family from the devastations of the drug nightmare. Our lives and the lives of those who stood in agreement with us are marked by a vigilant fight of faith that enabled us to withstand, stand, and stand therefore to see the salvation of our God.

HOW IT ALL BEGAN

Looking back over my life, there were times it resembled a giant puzzle. Some pieces just naturally fit together. The challenge came with those pieces that looked like they should have fit, but when an attempt was made to connect, a misfit was soon evident. Let's start with the easy pieces...

I grew up in Memphis, Tennessee during the 1960's. My parents were hard-working, no non-sense type of people. My father worked two jobs – a machine operator in a paper plant by day and by night (depending upon which shift he worked) and an auto mechanic on the weekends. My mother worked standing on her feet all day in the sweltering heat of a commercial laundry and still managed to prepare a hot cooked meal for her family every day. There were four girls growing up (my two brothers came along later) and we were always neat, clean, and well-dressed. It was such a treat for us to ride the bus downtown and meet my mother for a shopping spree.

Having little education themselves and struggling all of their lives to make a decent living (from the cotton fields in Mississippi to the plants in Memphis), my parents instilled in us the importance of getting a good education. In that respect, I was the golden child – always an honor roll student, played the piano, directed the high school gospel choir (which won the state championship by the way), and received numerous academic awards and scholarships; excelling in all my endeavors. Within me was a burning desire to achieve, to win, and to make my parents proud. Well, one summer day...

One of my neighbors was Mitchell Stewart's girlfriend at the time and she introduced us. I recall our first conversation in which he literally sized me up with these words – "little girl." Wanting desperately to prove that I was not a little girl, I retorted, "I'm going to high school." Somehow this statement did not generate the positive response that I expected. He thought it was quite funny; so I could hardly wait until the first day of school, to run him down in the hallway, and to prove him wrong. The fight was on! Could these two opposites possibly attract? We were so different. He worked a job, attended school, and owned a car. I worked full-time as an honor student. He was popular with the girls. I had a boyfriend who was afraid to even hold my hand. He fought his fights. I ran from mine. It seemed like I was always getting beat up by the bullies at school, my big sister at home. I was the one who was always running. Now here it is our wedding day, mine and Mitchell's, and wouldn't you know it – another fight!

His ex-girlfriend was on the front porch of our duplex, making threats and shouting obscenities. My long-awaited honeymoon was interrupted by a fight between my husband and his ex-girlfriend! I could hardly believe what was happening. What had I gotten myself into this time?

I had fallen in love with Mitchell Stewart almost immediately after that first time when he dared to call me a little girl. We were in the high school gospel choir and spending more time together, participating in choir activities. His parents were faithful supporters and always present for our performances. At one particular choir event, I became ill just after leading a song. It was Mitchell Stewart who picked me up in his arms, carried me out of the church, took me to the emergency room, and never left my side.

Not long after that, Mitchell and Brenda were officially "going together." As passions increased, the controls decreased. "She's pregnant." I can still hear the obstetrician's words as he told my mother that I was pregnant at age 17. Surely not me! Voted *"Most Likely to Succeed"* in junior high school, I left the doctor's office that day feeling like I was *"Most Likely to Fail."* Instead of preparing to attend college in the Fall of 1976 on an academic scholarship to a private university, I was preparing to give birth in February 1977.

"I'm not ready to get married." When I heard those words from my high school sweetheart, the love of my life, the father of my son, I was devastated. Nevertheless, I refused to settle for anything less than marriage. He was committed to taking care of his financial responsibilities, but he wanted no part of any marital responsibilities. I had envisioned life with Mitchell, and now I had to move on to life without Mitchell. I got a job. I became employed with the county hospital administration as a Receptionist and received several promotions during my tenure: Administrative Secretary to the Medical Director and Administrative Secretary to the Vice-President of Hospital Administration.

Well, he had a change of heart ten months later. On December 20, 1977, I married Mitchell B. Stewart, Sr. and I realized why I loved him. He always took care of things. He held a job, worked hard, managed the money, and always took care of his family.

When his employer closed its operation in Memphis, he secured another job with the same company and moved us to Houston, Texas. Shortly afterward, he found himself unemployed again, but I had found a job, so we decided to stay. He eventually secured a position with a major global carrier, making more money than he had ever made before, along with great benefits. Things were so good that I was able to quit my job and stay home with our four children. We bought a home in Spring, Texas; became members of a Bible-believing, Bible-teaching church; life was grand! So, I thought.

THE FIGHT OF MY LIFE

The bottom fell out of our marriage when I learned from my husband that he was addicted to crack-cocaine. In that same hour, I learned that our house note was three months behind and our cars were about to be repossessed. I was a young mother, happy at home raising our family, and had never fought a fight a day in my life. Little did I know I was in for the fight of my life! Not only for my own life, but for the life of my husband, and for the lives of our four children!

Many of the lessons that I learned from this life-changing experience are shared within the pages of this book. Lessons that I have now come to realize were not just for this particular bout, but lessons that I would live by for the rest of my life. This is my personal story of how God walked me though the discovery, the desire, the decision, the determination, and the self-defining moments that impacted and influenced my fight.   It is my hope that through my testimony, you will be encouraged to seek God's perfect will concerning your deployment strategies, to recognize the difference (if any) in your particular situation, and that one day, you too will be able to tell your story as the demonstration of His Glory. It's time to get *"FIT FOR THE FIGHT!"*

ROUND 1
THE DISCOVERY

GOING INTO THE RING WITH AN UNKNOWN OPPONENT

"What you don't know can't hurt you." Whoever made this statement must not have read the part in Hosea 4:6 that says, "My people are destroyed for lack of knowledge"...What I did not know about relationships was not only hurting my marriage, it was destroying my marriage! I needed to know what to do in order to set on a positive course a relationship that had taken a negative turn.

I found my answers in the best-selling Manual - The Bible, a textbook that provided the guidelines for all types of relationship, a rulebook that was given under the instructions of the Master of Relationships, God Himself. I became a serious student of the Word of God, searching to see if it was so. I was hungry for the knowledge of what to do (the tools) and the understanding of how to do it (the techniques). And there it was, right there in His Book; not the way it was, but the way it should be: each partner functioning according to their God-given purpose, working together to achieve the end-result of a relationship that is mutually fulfilling to all of the involved parties. It sounded good, but was it possible for this relationship?

Now that I had discovered the truth, I was willing to align myself with that truth, but what about my husband? How were we going to get into harmony with God's order for our marriage? To make matters worse, we were dealing with another factor – My husband was addicted to crack-cocaine. How were we going to address this misbehavior?

For clarification purposes, the term "misbehavior" (as used in this book) is defined as any behavior that is contrary to the expressed Will of God. For example: any form of abuse - physical, verbal, mental, substance, rebellion, disobedience, and disrespect.

Not only was I lacking in information about marriage, I didn't know anything about crack-cocaine. I am now in the ring with two opponents. Yes, me - one who hadn't won a fight yet!

In order to disarm my opponent, I needed to know his strategy. This simple truth concerning the make-up of mankind helped me to identify the opponent (Satan) and the opponent's strategy (a crack-cocaine addiction assigned to destroy the Stewart household).

UNDERSTANDING THE MAKE-UP OF MAN

> Now may the God of peace Himself sanctify you completely; and may your whole spirit, soul, and body be preserved blameless at the coming of our Lord Jesus Christ.
>
> I Thessalonians 5:23

Man is a tripartite-being (spirit, soul, and body). You are a spirit being, you live inside a physical body, and you possess a soul. The soul is the mind, the will, the imagination, the emotions, and the intellect. Every man has a will and the will is like the door, the gatekeeper, the guard over your behavior room. Here's a word of caution: The will is not to be violated! The will is to be influenced and impacted. A person persuaded against their will is of the same persuasion still.

Now Satan attempts to anesthetize the will through the use of drugs, alcohol, or immorality in an attempt to gain access to the spirit. Whichever is the stronger, the spirit or the body, ultimately influences the will of man to obey or disobey God. These four (4) spiritual principles of behavior fortified me for the fight:

1. WHAT DO YOU SAY?

> So Jesus answered and said to them, "Have faith in God. 23 For assuredly, I say to you, whoever says to this mountain, 'Be removed and be cast into the sea,' and does not doubt in his heart, but believes that those things he says will be done, he will have whatever he says. 24 Therefore I say to you, whatever things you ask when you pray, believe that you receive them, and you will have them. 25 "And whenever you stand praying, if you have anything against anyone, forgive him, that your Father in heaven may also forgive you your trespasses.
>
> Mark 11:22-25

CONFESSION BRINGS POSSESSION

My four children were my best warriors. They learned through standing in faith for their father's deliverance to put pressure on their tongues and to speak in agreement with the Word of God in spite of what they saw, in spite of what they heard, and in spite of how they felt. During the times that my husband was away from the home, when others would ask where their father was, my children would respond, "He is delivered". They said it so much that the children in the neighborhood thought that their father lived in "Delivered."

2. WHO IS ALLOWED TO SPEAK INTO YOUR EAR?

> Do not be unequally yoked together with unbelievers. For what fellowship has righteousness with lawlessness? And what communion has light with darkness?
>
> II Corinthians 6:14

GUARDING YOUR ASSOCIATIONS

- **Bible-believing, Bible-teaching church** – Yes, where you go to church matters! My church taught me the principles of the God-Kind of Faith, straight from the Word of God, in a simple, easy-to-understand-format so that I was able to hear it, understand it, and apply it in my everyday life. It was my faith which enabled me to win this fight.

- **Support Group** – I attended a weekly addiction recovery session led by a couple in my church that had overcome drug addiction. It was so important for me to see what the end-result of my faith could look like – Would we (Mitchell & Brenda Stewart) stand before others and tell our story one day?

- **Employer** – God gave me tremendous favor with my employer. When local and national vendors would bring the Houston Division President holiday gifts, sample products, tickets to sports events, you name it – I got it! When the employees requested a Bible Study during the lunch hour, I was approved to be the Bible Study Teacher and allowed to use the corporate conference rooms. When I resigned from the company to go to work for my church, the President himself asked me to reconsider; even offering me another job in the company.

- **Immediate Family** – Our family members (mine and my husband's) were fully supportive, assisting with the needs for food, clothing, shelter, school supplies, even an occasional trip home to see family in Memphis. Even though it was painful for them to see us go through this challenging time, they respected my decision to stay in Houston, and fight the enemy on the same turf that he started the fight.

- **Extended Family** – We faced what appeared to be insurmountable financial challenges. With no money for daycare, I decided to allow my youngest daughter to live in Memphis with family. Having my child separated from me just seemed like one battle the enemy had won. Oh, but God! He raised up a couple who came to me and asked if they could help. The wife, a Christian and the public affairs director for my employer, was aware of my situation. She and her husband were faithful to not only pay the daycare costs in full the first of every month for several years, but also blessed my children with gifts, and gave my husband a job.

3. **WHAT ACTIONS DO YOU TAKE TO GET IN SHAPE FOR THE FIGHT?**

Imitate me, just as I also imitate Christ.

I Corinthians 11:1

TAKE ACTION ON PURPOSE

God had given me what I needed for my spiritual growth and development in the form of role models, mentors, teachers, and living examples of Godly men and women who were committed to a righteous lifestyle in word and in deeds. It's my turn; so what would I do with all that I had received? After all, I had a history of following someone else's lead, conforming to someone else's expectations - but not this time. I had discovered a truth that no one could take away from me. God was not expecting me to be a carbon copy of someone else. God had done a new thing in me and He was expecting ME to show up for the fight! *(You can read more about ME in Round 5)*

BECOMING A SIGNIFICANT OTHER

In Genesis chapter 17, when God changed the name of "Abram" to "Abraham", He also changed the name of "Sarai" to "Sarah". The name change was necessary for both of them because they were partners in faith. I believed the same thing to be true for us. I was calling my husband a new name - "Delivered;" so I needed to call myself a new name - "Significant Other." The term "Significant Other" (as used in this book) is defined as a person committed to standing in faith for God's perfect will to come to pass for someone else.

As a Significant Other, I assumed a new role with two primary responsibilities:

A. <u>To walk in spiritual authority</u>

Then the seventy returned with joy, saying, "Lord, even the demons are subject to us in Your name." 18 And He said to them, "I saw Satan fall like lightning from heaven. 19 Behold, I give you the authority to trample on serpents and scorpions, and

over all the power of the enemy, and nothing shall
by any means hurt you.

Luke 10:17-19

Did this scripture really mean that I had been given the
power (authority in the Name of Jesus) over all of the power
(ability) of the enemy and there was nothing that the enemy
could do to hurt me? Because so far, the devil had done a
good job of hurting me. I heard Luke 10:19, believed it,
received it, and acted on it. Well, it was Luke 10:19 that set
me free and free indeed. The weapons did not stop forming.
The weapons stopped prospering. And I knew why. I got the
power!

B. To intercede before God on behalf of someone else

So I sought for a man among them who would
make a wall, and stand in the gap before Me on
behalf of the land, that I should not destroy it; but I
found no one.

Ezekiel 22:30

It was as if God Himself was speaking directly to me.
Will you stand for Mitchell Stewart to keep him alive long
enough for him to "come to himself?" Will you help to turn
back the impending destruction of drug addiction? Can I
count on you?

4. WHO IS YOUR HEAD TRAINER?

Then Jesus answered and said: "A certain man went down from Jerusalem to Jericho, and fell among thieves, who stripped him of his clothing, wounded him, and departed, leaving him half dead. 31 Now by chance a certain priest came down that road. And when he saw him, he passed by on the other side. 32 Likewise a Levite, when he arrived at the place, came and looked, and passed by on the other side. 33 But a certain Samaritan, as he journeyed, came where he was. And when he saw him, he had compassion. 34 So he went to him and bandaged his wounds, pouring on oil and wine; and he set him on his own animal, brought him to an inn, and took care of him. 35 On the next day, when he departed, he took out two denarii, gave them to the innkeeper, and said to him, 'Take care of him; and whatever more you spend, when I come again, I will repay you.' 36 So which of these three do you think was neighbor to him who fell among the thieves?"

37 And he said, "He who showed mercy on him." Then Jesus said to him, "Go and do likewise.

Luke 10:30-37

SURROUND YOURSELVES WITH THE VERY BEST COACHES OR TRAINERS. BE ACCOUNTABLE TO SOMEONE WHO HAS YOUR BEST INTEREST.

God had brought me into the company of men and women of faith and power who were willing to sacrifice of their time, their talent, and their treasure for the work of the ministry and they did so by:

1) **<u>Rearranging their schedules</u>** – They had won their battle over addictions, but came back to give back to those of us who needed to be encouraged in our faith fight. They had something else to do, somewhere else to go, but instead of passing by on the other side, they made it their business to be present every week to remind us that God would do the "same thing" for us that He had done for them.

2) **<u>Rendering some service</u>** - Most of my calls for help would have been considered "inconvenient" to someone else, but not to those called to this "ministry of inconvenience". They came when I called, they attended to my immediate needs, they stabilized me, and then they brought me to the place that provided the next level of care.

3) **<u>Releasing some silver</u>** - Through the hands of the coaches, trainers, mentors, and countless others, God overwhelmed me, far beyond what I could ask or think, exceeded my imagination, that's how the blessings came. I recall one holiday meal box that should have been enough for one day, that one meal box supernaturally provided meals for not only me and my four children, but it also fed three out-of-town houseguests.

4) And because they rearranged schedules, rendered service, and released silver, every person that allowed

God to utilize them in the building of Team Mitchell & Brenda Stewart, every person is therefore entitled to **receive a Godly reward**.

ROUND 2
THE DESIRE

In the preparation stages of the fight, thoughts of doubt and unbelief came to my mind, but those negative thoughts were not granted entrance into my spirit. The spirit is the real you, the center, the core, the heart. How do things get into your spirit? By what you hear, what you see, and what you say.

> My son, give attention to my words; Incline your ear to my sayings. 21 Do not let them depart from your eyes; Keep them in the midst of your heart; 22 For they are life to those who find them, And health to all their flesh.23 Keep your heart with all diligence, For out of it spring the issues of life.
>
> Proverbs 4:20-23

I was confessing daily, speaking faith-filled words out of my mouth, making this statement of faith: "My husband is delivered from crack-cocaine." My fight would have been over before it ever got started had I allowed things that were not in agreement with my statement of faith to get into my spirit.

I believed that I was doing the right thing and for the right reasons. Initially, I just wanted my husband to be free of drug addictions, to love God, to love me, and to love our children. That was my version of "happily ever after" until God revealed something that I had not considered.

God told me that His desire for Mitchell Stewart, Sr. was for him to walk in his deliverance; not because he was my husband, but because he was God's child.

> Therefore if the Son makes you free, you shall be free indeed.
>
> John 8:36

The Blood that Jesus Christ shed on Calvary has set us free from the powers of darkness and we are free indeed. There is power in the Name of Jesus to break every chain, tear down every stronghold, release every hostage, destroy every yoke of bondage, and set every captive free.

I believed that no child of God should be enslaved; therefore, in the authority of the Name of Jesus, I began to command the demonic forces to loose my husband and let him go! God had a work for him to do, a calling that he needed to answer, a divine assignment with his name on it. And for that reason, I prayed more fervently, "Father, not my will, but let your will be done."

ROUND 3
THE DECISION

WHAT IS A TOUGH LOVE DECISION?

The Decision to Fight is a tough love decision. It is a quality decision to maintain a mental toughness in spite of any temporary discomfort, temporary displeasure, temporary persecution or temporary pressure to compromise the Word of God. The key was to bear in mind that these things (the discomfort, the displeasure, the persecution, and the pressure) were all "temporary."

> For which of you, intending to build a tower, does not sit down first and count the cost, whether he has enough to finish it— 29 lest, after he has laid the foundation, and is not able to finish, all who see it begin to mock him, 30 saying, 'This man began to build and was not able to finish?'
>
> Luke 14:28-30

Since a quality decision is not an emotional decision, it is wisdom to first sit down (take a seat and allow your emotions to settle down) and then count the cost (what will be necessary for a "marvel" and not a "mockery.") Otherwise, you become sensual, sense-ruled, and sense-controlled. Now I heard that, I believed that, and I had good intentions to do that, but one day... My husband was struggling with staying free. He would do well for a period of time and then relapse.

In the heat of anger, my frustrations came out one day with these words, "Go to hell!" He ran to the telephone, dialed our Pastor's number, told him what I had said, and gave me the telephone. My Pastor's words still echo in my ears to this day, "Brenda, did you tell Mitchell to go to hell? We're trying to keep Mitchell out of hell." I should have sat down first.

WHEN YOU MAKE A QUALITY DECISION, YOU CAN EXPECT IT TO DO FOUR (4) THINGS:

1. **To give direction and purpose to your life**

2. **To take care of a lot of other decisions**

3. **To be the first step toward a significant goal, and**

4. **To bring structure, order and discipline to your life**

One quality decision all of us should make is to make Jesus Lord and Savior according to Romans 10:9-10.

> That if you confess with your mouth the Lord Jesus and believe in your heart that God has raised Him from the dead, you will be saved. 10 For with the heart one believes unto righteousness, and with the mouth confession is made unto salvation.
>
> Romans 10:9-10

The next quality decision that all born-again Believers should make is to be filled with the Holy Spirit according to Acts 1:8. The Holy Spirit empowers your prayer life, empowers your praise life, and empowers your personal life.

> But you shall receive power when the Holy Spirit has come upon you; and you shall be witnesses to Me in Jerusalem, and in all Judea and Samaria, and to the end of the earth."
>
> Acts 1:8

After receiving salvation and the indwelling power of the Holy Spirit, it is a quality decision to become an active member of a Bible-believing, Bible-teaching, Bible-living church so that you can mature spiritually in the things of God.

> And let us consider one another in order to stir up love and good works, 25 not forsaking the assembling of ourselves together, as is the manner of some, but exhorting one another, and so much the more as you see the Day approaching.
>
> Hebrews 10:24-25

THE FIGHT DECISION IS A COMBINATION OF THREE THINGS:

1. WHAT THE WORD OF GOD SAYS ABOUT THE SITUATION +

2. THE DISCIPLINE TO STAND ON WHAT THE WORD OF GOD SAYS +

3. THE UNCONDITIONAL LOVE FOR THE PERSON.

ROUND 4
THE DETERMINATION

Then He said: "A certain man had two sons. 12 And the younger of them said to his father, 'Father, give me the portion of goods that falls to me.' So he divided to them his livelihood. 13 And not many days after, the younger son gathered all together, journeyed to a far country, and there wasted his possessions with prodigal living. 14 But when he had spent all, there arose a severe famine in that land, and he began to be in want. 15 Then he went and joined himself to a citizen of that country, and he sent him into his fields to feed swine. 16 And he would gladly have filled his stomach with the pods that the swine ate, and no one gave him anything. 17 "But when he came to himself, he said, 'How many of my father's hired servants have bread enough and to spare, and I perish with hunger! 18 I will arise and go to my father, and will say to him, "Father, I have sinned against heaven and before you, 19 and I am no longer worthy to be called your son. Make me like one of your hired servants."' 20 "And he arose and came to his father. But when he was still a great way off, his father saw him and had compassion, and ran and fell on his neck and kissed him. 21 And the son said to him, 'Father, I have sinned against heaven and in your sight, and am no longer worthy to be called your son.'

22 "But the father said to his servants, 'Bring out the best robe and put it on him, and put a ring on his

hand and sandals on his feet. 23 And bring the fatted calf here and kill it, and let us eat and be merry; 24 for this my son was dead and is alive again; he was lost and is found.' And they began to be merry.

Luke 15:11-24

The Parable of the Lost Son in Luke chapter 15 is one of the greatest biblical models of the tough love decision and that is why this passage quickly became one of my favorites. An ungrateful son squanders his father's wealth, becomes an embarrassment to the family name, finally gets his act together and then wants to come back home? Where did the father in this story get the determination to stand in faith, the entire duration of his son's misbehavior, not knowing when it would end?

It has been said that a person's attitude will determine their altitude. The father in the parable must have had a New Attitude! In a Tough Love Stand, a firm mental attitude is critical in order to be strong like iron, mixed with the components of faith, love and discipline, for a steel-like disposition, a temperament that would:

1. **Be firm, but flexible**

2. **Yield to external forces without breaking, and**

3. **Be capable of resisting great strain without coming apart.**

That is exactly what the father was doing when he allowed his son to have a Pig Pen Experience (PPE). The father was determined to live in daily expectation of his son returning home. (The ring, the robe, and the shoes were already in the house. The calf was already fattened in preparation for the homecoming.) The father was determined not to interfere. The father was determined not to interrupt. The father was determined not to rescue.

The father had the determination and was able to maintain a firm, mental attitude because he understood that his son would eventually come to a point of decision and change for one of two reasons: for pain or for pleasure. When the pain of the PPE became unbearable for the son, he recalled the pleasures of the father's house, he came to himself and he said, "I will arise and go to my father, and say to him…"

Brenda would have to allow Mitchell to have a Pig Pen Experience (PPE). Brenda would have to be determined to live in daily expectation of Mitchell's homecoming. Brenda would have to be determined not to interfere, not to interrupt, and not to rescue. And when the pain of the "PPE" would become unbearable, Mitchell would recall the pleasures of the Father's house, he would arise, he would come to himself, go to the Father, and say to Him, "I've sinned…"

ROUND 5
THE DEFINING SELF

My weekly addiction recovery session proved to be an invaluable resource of natural and spiritual information. It was in this learning environment that I came face-to-face with the root cause of why I had been so tolerant of my husband's misbehavior. Low self-esteem was the culprit.

I did not see myself as worthy, good enough, or valuable in and of myself. In order to win this fight, that would have to change! It was going to take strong self-esteem to be able to effectively confront my husband; something I had been unable to do in the past. That was before I became acquainted with II Samuel chapters 11-12.

In II Samuel chapter 11, at a time when kings go out to battle, King David (from his rooftop) chose to "look" and then "took" Bathsheba, the wife of Uriah the Hittite. Bathsheba became pregnant with David's child, but returned to Uriah's house. To cover-up his mess-up, David made several unsuccessful, strategic attempts to get Uriah to sleep with Bathsheba, but Uriah's integrity was simply impeccable. Therefore King David wrote a letter to the captain of his army and sent that letter by the hand of Uriah. And he wrote in the letter, saying, "Set Uriah in the forefront of the hottest battle, and retreat from him, that he may be struck down and die."

An adulterer and a murderer, King David proceeded with business as usual, as if nothing had happened. After the customary mourning period was over, at liberty to do what was considered the right thing, King David married Uriah's widow and a son was born. And they lived happily ever after? No, because the thing that David had done displeased God.

In II Samuel chapter 12, God loved David too much to allow him to continue covering up his sin, so God sent the Prophet Nathan to confront King David for the purpose of:

1. Compelling David to come face-to-face with what he had done;

2. Giving David the opportunity to come to himself and repent; and

3. Allowing David to experience the consequences of his own misbehavior.

"Was I ready to do what the Prophet Nathan had done with King David? An effective confrontation would require self-evaluation to ensure that I was spiritually prepared to:

1) **Fight the good fight of faith**, to go the distance, until he desired to change.

Would I stand in faith for his deliverance no matter how long it would take for him "to come to himself?"

> Fight the good fight of faith, lay hold on eternal life, to which you were also called and have confessed

the good confession in the presence of many witnesses.

I Timothy 6:12

2) **Enforce the consequences.** Was I prepared to implement the plan of action if he refused to alter his ways? The same God that put the man in the Garden of Eden (Genesis 2:15), is also the same God that drove the man out of the Garden of Eden (Genesis 3:24) Things were constantly coming up missing; like the refrigerator. Well, we had two. He didn't see anything wrong with giving away one. Who did you give it to? A charitable organization. I called that charitable organization and was told they did not take refrigerators. His response – They took that one. I told my husband the next time something leaves this house, you will leave too. So when my sister's engagement ring mysteriously came up missing, that was his next time and his time to go.

3) **Place emotional restraints on myself;** not allowing my emotions to overwhelm me and cause me to compromise my stand. My love for my husband and the desire to see God's perfect will come to pass in his life were motivating factors to toughen up emotionally and take a tough love stand. My eyes could see the physical toll that the drug addiction was taking on him - the drastic weight loss, the unkempt appearance; he

looked like a walking dead man. The sight of his physical being would have caused me to break down, to feel helpless and hopeless had it not been for the spiritual light of God's Word shining through in these two passages.

> While we do not look at the things which are seen, but at the things which are not seen. For the things which are seen are temporary, but the things which are not seen are eternal.

II Corinthians 4:18

> For we walk by faith, not by sight.

II Corinthians 5:7

3)   Commit to prayer.

> Confess your trespasses to one another, and pray for one another, that you may be healed. The effective, fervent prayer of a righteous man avails much.

James 5:16

NOT ONLY WAS I PRAYING FOR MY HUSBAND, BUT I ENLISTED THE SUPPORT OF FAMILY, FRIENDS, CO-WORKERS, CHURCH MEMBERS AND OTHERS IN THE BODY OF CHRIST. PEOPLE WHO DIDN'T EVEN KNOW US WERE OFFERING HEARTFELT PRAYERS FOR MITCHELL STEWART.

And why do you look at the speck in your brother's eye, but do not consider the plank in your own eye? 4 Or how can you say to your brother, 'Let me remove the speck from your eye'; and look, a plank is in your own eye? 5 Hypocrite! First remove the plank from your own eye, and then you will see clearly to remove the speck from your brother's eye.

Matthew 7:3-5

Before confronting the other person, first examine yourself to see if there are things that you might need to change and then develop a plan of action to work on those things. But isn't this confrontation about the other person's misbehavior? Why am I under personal attack? In an attempt to deflect attention from his misbehavior, my husband would bring up my shortcomings during a confrontation. "You're not perfect. You did this and you did that..." A good answer is, "I'm working to change my this and my that, but right now this conversation is about yours."

(5) DYNAMICS OF AN EFFECTIVE CONFRONTATION

1) **Tell the truth in love.**

2) **Have a compassion for God's best.** It may not necessarily be your way, but it should always be God's way.

3) **Choose the best method of confrontation.** You may need to write a letter first as a set-up for the face-to-face confrontation.

4) **Rehearse before you have a face-to-face confrontation and include these two pointers:**

- Use a sensitive story to help the person relate to you, to identify with your concern, to understand how you feel. Sensitive stories utilize the other person's sensitivities (their interests, hobbies, career) to make an emotional impact on them, so study the person and use creativity. In II Samuel 12:1-7, the Prophet Nathan used the biblical principle of meditation (words, images, and emotions) to appeal to the shepherd's heart in King David and before he knew it, David had pronounced his own death sentence. The Hebrew word for "meditate" means to speak with oneself, to mutter, to ponder, to study. The Greek word for "meditate" means to take care of beforehand, to attend to carefully, to be diligent in, to reckon inwardly, to weigh the reasons of (to think upon), to deliberate.

- State the consequences that you intend to implement. No idle threats. Say what you mean and mean what you say.

5) **Take down your opponent.** Prepare for a knock out! Disarm the enemy's strategies against you. Present options to your loved one. The person's response can be to accept it and agree to change or the person can rebel and counterattack. If the person's unwilling to

change, be prepared to do whatever you said you would do.

- Failure to obey spiritual principles of behavior (how to act) will cause misbehavior. Misbehavior is simply behavior that is missed. Well what about the devil? Remember, the devil cannot take place; he has to be given place!

- All misbehavior (behavior that's missed) should be rewarded with consequences. Definition of consequences - The penalties imposed for misbehavior and what your response will be to misbehavior.

- When Clear Instructions/Clear Guidelines have been disobeyed or disregarded, then Clear Consequences/Clear Penalties have to be implemented in order for there to be a Clear Plan for Restoration / Reconciliation. Is that Clear?

ROUND 6
THE DEPLOYMENT STRATEGIES

We were down to one vehicle and I had been stranded so many times; waiting for him to take me to work, waiting for him to pick me up from work. One time my husband was trying to get the car keys from me, but I was not giving in. He had never done any physical harm to me before, so I was not afraid of him. He just wouldn't back down this time. He kept on badgering me to give him the car keys. Before I knew what was happening, he grabbed the sheet off of the bed, folded me into the sheet, tied me up like a package, and left me scrambling around on the floor. "I'll be right back..."

It was time to make a change. I was not the blame for his choices, but I accepted my responsibility to implement the consequences for his misbehavior. I had the ability to respond and I did so with a simple three-step plan of action that included:

1. **Assigning full responsibility for the misbehavior to him**

   a) Allowing consequences; no rescue.

   b) Establishing guidelines; no excuses.

    c) Investigating options; no delays.

2. **Bringing him to a point of decision realizing that:**

    a) His response could be accept and change.

    b) His response could be rebel and counter-attack.

    c) Whatever his response, I was prepared with my response.

3. **Giving him loving intervention**

    a) Reassured him of my love.

    b) Reassured him that I would not continue "as is."

ROUND 7
THE DIFFERENCE

In the fight world, there are so many variables that can affect the outcome of a match - the physical and mental condition of the fighters, the number of rounds, the weight class, the number of punches thrown, the number of punches landed and the list goes on. And likewise, so goes on the fight of faith for those who have yet to "come to themselves".

What made the difference for me? In March of 1992, Mitchell Stewart "came to himself." He completed a 90-day addiction recovery program in San Antonio, Texas. He called me on Day 90 and asked to come home. I was not ready and told him so. His response was to stay in San Antonio, get a job, and send money home to take care of his family. I knew he was free.

The results of the fight are decided when an opponent is deemed incapable of continuing by a referee, is disqualified for breaking a rule, resigns from the fight by throwing in a towel, or is pronounced the winner or the loser based on the judges' scorecards.

Before you declare your faith fight a defeat, before you conclude that your tough love stand has been a failure, please give prayerful consideration to this one thing – Is the person that you are standing in faith for still physically alive? If your answer is "yes", then the fight for their deliverance is not over!

If your relationship suffered a death as a direct result of the misbehavior and you chose to move on without the other person, keep praying, keep interceding, keep believing that one day, they "come to themselves". Jesus has not given up on us; therefore, we should not give up on one another. The Scripture below reiterates this important truth:

> Therefore He is also able to save to the uttermost those who come to God through Him, since He always lives to make intercession for them.
>
> Hebrews 7:25

ROUND 8
THE DEMONSTRATION

WITHSTAND, STAND, STAND THEREFORE

Finally, my brethren, be strong in the Lord and in the power of His might. 11 Put on the whole armor of God, that you may be able to stand against the wiles of the devil. 12 For we do not wrestle against flesh and blood, but against principalities, against powers, against the rulers of the darkness of this age, against spiritual hosts of wickedness in the heavenly places. 13 Therefore take up the whole armor of God, that you may be able to withstand in the evil day, and having done all, to stand. Stand therefore, having girded your waist with truth, having put on the breastplate of righteousness, 15 and having shod your feet with the preparation of the gospel of peace; 16 above all, taking the shield of faith with which you will be able to quench all the fiery darts of the wicked one. 17 And take the helmet of salvation, and the sword of the Spirit, which is the word of God; 18 praying always with all prayer and supplication in the Spirit, being watchful to this end with all perseverance and supplication for all the saints—

Ephesians 6:10-18

"Withstand, Stand, and Stand Therefore" became my Fight Song. It was my "1-2-3 Punch" and my best attempt at an explanation was:

I had faced a giant and in spite of the initial impact of that encounter, did not retreat, but advanced <u>even though trembling</u> – **WITHSTAND.**

I had become a serious student of the Word of God, meditating in it day and night, observing to do all that it commanded me to do, and my faith <u>endured the test</u> – **STAND.**

I was empowered by the Holy Spirit, fully persuaded by the faithfulness of God who had kept His promise to never leave me and to never forsake me, and <u>experienced the triumph</u> – **STAND THEREFORE.**

Thank God that I had put on the whole armor of God:

HELMET OF SALVATION – THE CONCENTRATION.

Having confessed Jesus Christ as my personal Lord and Savior (according to Romans 10:9-10), I believed that Jesus was crucified on the cross for all our sins, was buried and resurrected, and is now seated at the right hand of the Father. His death gave us life - life eternally (living in heaven) and life abundantly (living on earth). Accepting this gracious gift placed me into God's family, with full covenant rights and benefits, no waiting period. I could depend on God to keep His promises as stated in His Word. That assurance alone was like a protective covering over my mind that helped me to stay focused and balanced, naturally and spiritually.

BREASTPLATE OF RIGHTEOUSNESS – THE CONVICTION.

Acknowledging that I was in right-standing with God made me worthy to go boldly to the throne of grace and ask for help in the time of trouble. I was in trouble – no place to live, no transportation, no money and overnight, I had become a single parent with four children, so add this one – no parental skills. Oh, but God! God had proven Himself to be my present help in the time of trouble. Now I know Who I Am (my identity), Whose I Am (my redeemer) and What I Am Entitled to Receive (my benefits).

BELT OF TRUTH – THE STRENGTH.

Recognizing that the truth of God's Word was the source of my spiritual strength set me free and free indeed. The truth supported me and held me steadfastly in place. I was willingly giving of my time, my talents, and my treasures for the work of the ministry and in return, God was supernaturally meeting every need – food, clothes, shelter. With an eviction notice on our apartment door, FEMA funds just happened to come into the assistance center that same day, and the rent was paid in full. Not my lucky day, but my blessed day! Yes, my joy did come in the morning and it came on the wings of truth.

FEET SHOD WITH THE PREPARATION OF THE GOSPEL OF PEACE – DIRECTION.

Submitting myself willingly, standing in all readiness to do God's perfect will, and allowing God's good pleasure did not all come about overnight, but developed over a period of time. God was speaking, but sometimes I was not listening. As my relationship with God matured, I learned how to recognize His voice. In spite of the learning curve, there was the peace of God that still surpasses my own understanding. We have come across drug dealers that my husband owed money and rather than an altercation, he was miraculously given a reprieve. Because we have committed ourselves fully to the Lord, He has kept us in perfect peace.

SWORD OF MY SPIRIT – ACTION.

Speaking the Word of God boldly out of my mouth required that I first take the time to hear it, to believe it, and to receive it. When Faith was being taught, I made it my business to be present. These were marvelous opportunities to learn how to respond in Faith. Faith comes by hearing. Faith is released by speaking. Faith works by love. It took time for us to dig ourselves into the hole we were in, and it was going to take time for us to dig ourselves out. It was not what I said (past) that would turn the situations around. It was not what I will say (future tense) that would change the circumstances. It was what I was saying (present); continuing to say. By continuing to speak the Word of God boldly out of my mouth, my faith was keeping my hope alive.

SHIELD OF FAITH – PROTECTION.

Understanding that the enemy is constant in his attack reinforced to me the need to be constant in my defense. Faith is like a fire extinguisher and it puts out every fiery dart (mental thought patterns) of the enemy. I had fought the good fight of faith and won, but there were no retirement plans for the armor. The justified or the declared righteous should live by faith. Faith is my lifestyle and not my life jacket. Faith is the only way to please God. I choose to please God; therefore I choose Faith. Faith is my plan for life and my plan for life is Faith.

And what good is the armor without the weapons?

For the weapons of our warfare are not carnal but mighty in God for pulling down strongholds,

II Corinthians 10:4

Just to name a few weapons:

FAITH - I JOHN 5:4

For whatever is born of God overcomes the world. And this is the victory that has overcome the world—our faith.

WORD OF GOD - HEBREWS 4:12

For the word of God is living and powerful, and sharper than any two-edged sword, piercing even to the division of soul and spirit, and of joints and marrow, and is a discerner of the thoughts and intents of the heart.

PRAYER - JAMES 5:16

Confess your trespasses to one another, and pray for one another, that you may be healed. The effective, fervent prayer of a righteous man avails much.

PRAISE AND WORSHIP - PSALMS 50:23

Whoever offers praise glorifies Me; And to him who orders his conduct a right, I will show the salvation of God.

FASTING - ISAIAH 58:5-6

Is it a fast that I have chosen, A day for a man to afflict his soul? Is it to bow down his head like a bulrush, And to spread out sackcloth and ashes? Would you call this a fast, And an acceptable day to the Lord? "Is this not the fast that I have chosen: To loose the bonds of wickedness, To undo the heavy burdens, To let the oppressed go free, And that you break every yoke?

AUTHORITY - LUKE 10:19

Behold, I give you the authority to trample on serpents and scorpions, and over all the power of the enemy, and nothing shall by any means hurt you.

BLOOD OF JESUS - REVELATION 12:11

And they overcame him by the blood of the Lamb and by the word of their testimony, and they did not love their lives to the death.

SPIRITUAL STAMINA - HEBREWS 10:35-36

Therefore do not cast away your confidence, which has great reward. 36 For you have need of endurance, so that after you have done the will of God, you may receive the promise:

The ability to Withstand, Stand, and Stand Therefore, to take my tough love stand, and to endure my faith battle all came when I stopped running in Fear, started operating in Faith, and subsequently became *"FIT FOR THE FIGHT!"*

PASTOR BRENDA STEWART
TOUGH LOVE
ON PAPER

13 LESSONS TO GET YOU

Fit

FOR THE

FIGHT!

THE VIGILANT FIGHT OF FAITH FOR MY HUSBAND, MY FAMILY, AND MYSELF

TOUGH LOVE ON PAPER (TLOP)

INTRODUCTION

"Tough Love on Paper" (TLOP) is my definition for the thirteen (13) lessons contained in the following section of this book. You have already read my testimony of how God delivered me, my husband, and my family. Now this section is devoted to the teaching of the Word without the testimony of Brenda Stewart. God is ready to perform His Word. Jeremiah 1:12 Then the LORD said to me, "You have seen well, for I am ready to perform My Word."

Are you ready for His Word to be performed in you? TLOP is a biblical roadmap, designed specifically for the Significant Other to know what to do to set on a positive course a relationship that has taken a negative turn.

When a User makes a quality decision to get free from addictive behaviors, the next step is a commitment to a recovery program that provides the tools (the knowledge) and the techniques (the application of the knowledge) necessary to walk in freedom. It has been proven that a habit can be broken within 21-30 days, but breaking it is not enough! Through my husband's experience, I am convinced that it takes another 30 days to form a new habit, and then another 30 days to fine-tune the newly formed habit.

When a Significant Other makes a tough love decision to stand in faith for the User, the next step is a commitment to a recovery program that provides the tools (the knowledge) and the techniques (the application of the knowledge) necessary to walk in freedom. It has been proven that a habit can be broken within 21-30 days, but breaking it is not enough! Through my personal experience, I am convinced that it takes another 30 days to form a new habit, and then another 30 days to fine-tune the newly formed habit.

Same thing? Yes, same thing. An effective, permanent change can occur for the User and the Significant Other within a 90-day-period. Significant Others, become a serious student, take one lesson per week and meditate on that particular lesson daily. If a key statement, principle, or truth is repeated from the previous section, then it is essential in helping you become fit for your fight. Remember, faith comes by hearing (by continuing to hear); not by having heard (She said that already).

Are you ready to position yourself for change? Let's begin with Lesson One of "Tough Love on Paper."

TOUGH LOVE ON PAPER (TLOP)

LESSON 1

The Parable of the Lost Son is a biblical model of the tough love principles that will be shared over the course of this teaching.

Then He said: "A certain man had two sons. 12 And the younger of them said to his father, 'Father, give me the portion of goods that falls to me.' So he divided to them his livelihood. 13 And not many days after, the younger son gathered all together, journeyed to a far country, and there wasted his possessions with prodigal living. 14 But when he had spent all, there arose a severe famine in that land, and he began to be in want. 15 Then he went and joined himself to a citizen of that country, and he sent him into his fields to feed swine. 16 And he would gladly have filled his stomach with the pods that the swine ate, and no one gave him anything.

17 "But when he came to himself, he said, 'How many of my father's hired servants have bread enough and to spare, and I perish with hunger! 18 I will arise and go to my father, and will say to him, "Father, I have sinned against heaven and before you, 19 and I am no longer worthy to be called your son. Make me like one of your hired servants."'

20 "And he arose and came to his father. But when he was still a great way off, his father saw him and had compassion, and ran and fell on his neck and kissed him. 21 And the son said to him, 'Father, I have sinned against heaven and in your sight, and am no longer worthy to be called your son.'

22 "But the father said to his servants, 'Bring out the best robe and put it on him, and put a ring on his hand and sandals on his feet. 23 And bring the fatted calf here and kill it, and let us eat and be merry; 24 for this my son was dead and is alive again; he was lost and is found.' And they began to be merry.

Luke 15:11-24

Behavior is defined as the manner in which we conduct ourselves. We can choose to behave or we can choose to misbehave. The willingness to obey the spiritual principles of behavior results in "good behavior", behavior that is compliant with the expressed Will of God (e.g. holiness, righteousness, obedience, self-control, goodness, respect). The failure to obey the spiritual principles of behavior results in "misbehavior", behavior that is contrary to the expressed Will of God (e.g. any form of abuse - physical, verbal, mental, substance [drugs and alcohol], sexual, rebellion, disobedience, disrespect). Misbehavior is simply behavior that is missed.

"The devil made me do it!" Ephesians 4:27 - nor give place to the devil. The devil cannot take place. We have to give him place. If you have given the devil a place (and he'll accept it if you give it to him), then cast him out. The Word of God does not say ask him out. It says cast him out!

> And these signs will follow those who believe: In My name they will cast out demons; they will speak with new tongues;
>
> Mark 16:17

You have just exercised your spiritual authority over the devil in the Name of Jesus. Now that he's gone (for a season), before he returns, get these powerful statements of truth into your spirit.

> Now may the God of peace Himself sanctify you completely; and may your whole spirit, soul, and body be preserved blameless at the coming of our Lord Jesus Christ.
>
> I Thessalonians 5:23

Man is a tripartite-being (spirit, soul, and body). You are a spirit being, you live inside a physical body, and you possess a soul. The soul is the mind, the will, the imagination, the emotions, and the intellect. Every man has the ability to set his will to believe or not to believe.

> Now Thomas, called the Twin, one of the twelve, was not with them when Jesus came. 25 The other disciples therefore said to him, "We have seen the Lord."

So he said to them, "Unless I see in His hands the print of the nails, and put my finger into the print of the nails, and put my hand into His side, I will not believe."

26 And after eight days His disciples were again inside, and Thomas with them. Jesus came, the doors being shut, and stood in the midst, and said, "Peace to you!" 27 Then He said to Thomas, "Reach your finger here, and look at My hands; and reach your hand here, and put it into My side. Do not be unbelieving, but believing."

28 And Thomas answered and said to Him, "My Lord and my God!" 29 Jesus said to him, "Thomas, because you have seen Me, you have believed. Blessed are those who have not seen and yet have believed."

John 20:24-29

The world says, "Seeing is believing." The Word says, "Believing is seeing." Believe that the righteous choices you make today affect not only you, but also generations to come.

I call heaven and earth as witnesses today against you, that I have set before you life and death, blessing and cursing; therefore choose life, that both you and your descendants may live; 20 that you may love the LORD your God, that you may obey His voice, and that you may cling to Him, for He is your life and the length of your days; and that you may dwell in the land which the LORD swore to your fathers, to Abraham, Isaac, and Jacob, to give them."

Deuteronomy 30:19-20

Believe that the righteous choices you make today are quality decisions.

> For which of you, intending to build a tower, does not sit down first and count the cost, whether he has enough to finish it— 29 lest, after he has laid the foundation, and is not able to finish, all who see it begin to mock him, 30 saying, 'This man began to build and was not able to finish?

Luke 14:28-30

Believe that the righteous choices you make today will outlast any temporary discomfort, temporary displeasure, temporary persecution or temporary pressure to compromise the Word of God.

> While we do not look at the things which are seen, but at the things which are not seen. For the things which are seen are temporary, but the things which are not seen are eternal.

II Corinthians 4:18

> For we walk by faith, not by sight.

II Corinthians 5:7

Tᴏᴜɢʜ Lᴏᴠᴇ Oɴ Pᴀᴘᴇʀ (TLOP)

LESSON 2

"But when he came to himself, he said, 'How many of my father's hired servants have bread enough and to spare, and I perish with hunger!"

Luke 15:17

The pain of the pigpen experience caused the son to "come to himself." He came to the realization that he was not himself. He reminisced about what life was like in his father's house. The servants had more than enough food, yet he (the son) was dying of starvation.

Meanwhile, back at the father's house, we are not told how long it took the son to come to himself, but we are told that he did. We can only imagine how life was for the father, living in daily expectation of his son returning home; not knowing when, not knowing how, but knowing any day now.

The father in Luke chapter 15 is representative of a "Significant Other." The term "Significant Other" (as used in this book) is defined as a person committed to standing in faith for God's perfect will to come to pass for someone else.

Then Jesus answered and said: "A certain man went down from Jerusalem to Jericho, and fell among thieves, who stripped him of his clothing, wounded him, and departed, leaving him half dead. 31 Now by chance a certain priest came down that road. And when he saw him, he passed by on the other side. 32 Likewise a Levite, when he arrived at the place, came and looked, and passed by on the other side. 33 But a certain Samaritan, as he journeyed, came where he was. And when he saw him, he had compassion. 34 So he went to him and bandaged his wounds, pouring on oil and wine; and he set him on his own animal, brought him to an inn, and took care of him. 35 On the next day, when he departed, he took out two denarii, gave them to the innkeeper, and said to him, 'Take care of him; and whatever more you spend, when I come again, I will repay you.' 36 So which of these three do you think was neighbor to him who fell among the thieves?" 37 And he said, "He who showed mercy on him." Then Jesus said to him, "Go and do likewise."

Luke 10:30-37

Significant Others demonstrate the care, the concern, and the compassion of Jesus to others by their willingness to:

- **Rearrange their schedules** – A certain Samaritan was on his way somewhere just like the Priest and the Levite. A certain Samaritan saw the same situation, but had compassion.

- **Render some service** – A certain Samaritan provided immediate care, using his own resources

- **Release some silver** – A certain Samaritan paid someone else to provide continued care and as a direct result of his actions, Jesus acknowledged a certain Samaritan as a "neighbor;" "one who showed mercy." This is a good example to follow, for those who are merciful are worthy to:

- **Receive a Godly reward** - Matthew 5:7 *Blessed are the merciful, for they shall obtain mercy.*

Significant Others, be on alert for Satan's attempts to interfere with your spiritual stamina, your spiritual strength by using these three weapons – Fear, Falsehood, and Fatigue.

Fear – Fear is not of God, so even if fear comes to your mind, just don't let it get into your heart by speaking it with your mouth. II Timothy 1:7 *For God has not given us a spirit of fear, but of power and of love and of a sound mind.*

Falsehood or Lies – John 8:44 *You are of your father the devil, and the desires of your father you want to do. He was a murderer from the beginning, and does not stand in the truth, because there is no truth in him. When he speaks a lie; he speaks from his own resources, for he is a liar and the father of it.*

Fatigue – II Chronicles 20:29-30 *And the fear of God was on all the kingdoms of those countries when they heard that the LORD had fought against the enemies of Israel. 30 Then the realm of Jehoshaphat was quiet, for his God gave him rest all around.*

The devil tries to wear you out physically, so make sure you get some rest. After you have fought the battle, gotten the victory, and received the spoils (the rewards from the battle), get some rest! Why? Because there's another battle on the way. After that battle, there is another victory. After that victory, there are more spoils. After the spoils, get some rest! And the cycle starts over again:

BATTLE– VICTORY– SPOILS – REST

TOUGH LOVE ON PAPER (TLOP)

LESSON 3

Powers of darkness are at work in the earth manipulating situations to keep Believers from experiencing God's best. Addictions are just one of the weapons used to steal, kill, and destroy lives.

How is the trap set?

> And they did not repent of their murders or their sorceries or their sexual immorality or their thefts.
>
> Revelation 9:21

> The light of a lamp shall not shine in you anymore, and the voice of bridegroom and bride shall not be heard in you anymore. For your merchants were the great men of the earth, for by your sorcery all the nations were deceived.
>
> Revelation 18:23

> But the cowardly, unbelieving, abominable, murderers, sexually immoral, ...idolaters, and all liars

shall have their part in the lake which burns with
fire...which is the second death.

Revelation 21:8

Drug addiction is a form of sorcery and witchcraft used
by the devil to manipulate and control mankind through the
abuse of substances. If the will (which is the guard over
behavior) is put to sleep through drug addiction, then the door
is open to all types of satanic influences. Pray for the Users
and Pray for the Dealers! Dealers are assisting in the control
and manipulation of others by enslaving them to drugs.

Who has taken this counsel against Tyre, the
crowning city, Whose merchants are princes, Whose
traders are the honorable of the earth?

Isaiah 23:8

Now that we have exposed drug addiction as a trick of
the enemy, what can be done to overcome its devastating
effects on the lives of men, women, children, and teenagers?

GET THE KNOWLEDGE

Be aware of the physical and spiritual symptoms
(denial, refusal to seek help, blaming others, withdrawal, lying,
deception, manipulation, stealing, behavioral and physical
changes, etc.)

Drug addiction is an iniquity (a sin) and to continue in
iniquity, to continue in sin will:

- ## Bring about destruction

  When the morning dawned, the angels urged Lot to hurry, saying, "Arise, take your wife and your two daughters who are here, lest you be consumed in the punishment of the city."

  Genesis 19:15

- ## Take away strength

  For my life is spent with grief, And my years with sighing; My strength fails because of my iniquity, And my bones waste away.

  Psalms 31:10

- ## Bring bondage and captivity

  Since the days of our fathers to this day we have been very guilty, and for our iniquities we, our kings, and our priests have been delivered into the hand of the kings of the lands, to the sword, to captivity, to plunder, and to humiliation, as it is this day.

  Ezra 9:7

God forgives iniquity. God forgives drug addiction.

For I will be merciful to their unrighteousness, and their sins and their lawless deeds I will remember no more."

Hebrews 8:12

Stand in Authority - For this purpose, Jesus came and made the works of the devil null and void, of no effect.

He who sins is of the devil, for the devil has sinned from the beginning. For this purpose the Son of God was manifested, that He might destroy the works of the devil.

I John 3:8

When we receive Jesus as our Savior and Lord according to Romans 10:9-10, we are given this spiritual authority simply because we are His sons and daughters! The Scripture in John 1:12 assures us of this:

But as many as received Him, to them He gave the right to become children of God, to those who believe in His name:

John 1:12

As a Significant Other, you have made a commitment to stand in faith for God's perfect will to come to pass for someone else. You stand in faith and you stand in authority. The devil has ability. The Believer has authority. Authority always supersedes ability. Luke 10:19

Behold, I give you the authority to trample on serpents and scorpions, and over all the power of the enemy, and nothing shall by any means hurt you.

Spiritual authority is released over the powers of darkness with the words of your mouth. Demonic forces are "cast" out, not "asked" out. Spiritual authority has been delegated to Believers in the Name of Jesus, and we can expect:

1. Demons to respect the Name of Jesus

2. Miracles to happen

3. Prayers to be answered, and

4. Greater works to be performed to God's Glory

TOUGH LOVE ON PAPER (TLOP)

LESSON 4

We are continuing in our answer to the question posed in Lesson Three: Now that we have exposed drug addiction as one of the tricks of the enemy, what can be done to overcome its devastating effects on the lives of men, women, children, and teenagers? Get the Knowledge, Stand in Authority and in today's lesson – Pray for the Drug User and Pray for the Drug Dealer.

> Confess your trespasses to one another, and pray for one another, that you may be healed. The effective, fervent prayer of a righteous man avails much.
>
> James 5:16

Pray for their salvation. If the person is not saved or unsure of their salvation, then lead them in a simple prayer for salvation. Have them repeat after you – "Dear God, I know that without Jesus, I am lost. I believe your Word that if I confess with my mouth the Lord Jesus and believe in my heart that God raised him from the dead, I shall be saved. I now invite you Jesus into my heart and receive you by faith as my Lord and Savior. Forgive me for my sins. Devil, you don't have me anymore. Jesus is my Lord. I am now a new creature in Christ and a child of God. Thank you, Father for saving me in Jesus name. Amen."

> That if you confess with your mouth the Lord Jesus and believe in your heart that God has raised Him from the dead, you will be saved. 10 For with the heart one believes unto righteousness, and with the mouth confession is made unto salvation.
>
> Romans 10:9-10

Pray that they renounce their allegiance to witchcraft. After salvation, have them repeat after you - "You foul demons of witchcraft, I renounce you and all of your control over my life. I command the powers of darkness to cease their activities in my life in the Name of Jesus. Jesus has set me free and I am free indeed! I stand in authority over all of the ability of the enemy and nothing shall be any means hurt or harm me. Jesus is my Lord and Savior and him only will I serve. I declare that I am free in Jesus Name."

> Therefore submit to God. Resist the devil and he will flee from you.
>
> James 4:7

Pray that the spiritual attack ceases. "In the Name of Jesus, I speak to the tormenting spirit of witchcraft and I command you to cease your attack in this person's life. I command every seducing spirit to come out of this person now. In the Name of Jesus, every stronghold is broken.

Blindfolds come off and the light of the glorious gospel shines through."

> But even if our gospel is veiled, it is veiled to those who are perishing, 4 whose minds the god of this age has blinded, who do not believe, lest the light of the gospel of the glory of Christ, who is the image of God, should shine on them.
>
> II Corinthians 4:3-4

Pray that the physical body heals. "In the Name of Jesus, The Word of God declares that by the stripes of Jesus you are healed. I command your body to function according to its God-given purpose. I speak to every muscle, cell, fiber, nerve, organ and bone in your body. I call you whole, complete, and sound in Jesus' Name."

> But He was wounded for our transgressions, He was bruised for our iniquities; The chastisement for our peace was upon Him, And by His stripes we are healed.
>
> Isaiah 53:5

Pray that they commit to a Bible-believing, Bible-teaching church and make the decision to grow spiritually. The church has been given revelation truth that can transform the lives of every person involved in the drug nightmare.

> Jesus answered and said to him, "Blessed are you, Simon Bar-Jonah, for flesh and blood has not revealed this to you, but My Father who is in

heaven. 18 And I also say to you that you are Peter, and on this rock I will build My church, and the gates of Hades shall not prevail against it. 19 And I will give you the keys of the kingdom of heaven, and whatever you bind on earth will be bound in heaven, and whatever you loose on earth will be loosed in heaven."

Matthew 16:17-19

TOUGH LOVE ON PAPER (TLOP)

LESSON 5

But be doers of the word, and not hearers only, deceiving yourselves. 23 For if anyone is a hearer of the word and not a doer, he is like a man observing his natural face in a mirror; 24 for he observes himself, goes away, and immediately forgets what kind of man he was. 25 But he who looks into the perfect law of liberty and continues in it, and is not a forgetful hearer but a doer of the work, this one will be blessed in what he does.

James 1:22-25

The next five lessons help to develop Your Esteem Statement (YES). What do you think of yourself, your worth, and purpose?

For as he thinks in his heart, so is he.

Proverbs 23:7a

To help you formulate your statement, each lesson will focus on a truth from the Word of God that we will utilize as a self-esteem builder. Today's self-esteem builder: I am fearfully and wonderfully made.

I will praise You, for I am fearfully and wonderfully made; Marvelous are Your works, And that my soul knows very well.

Psalm 139:14

I am fearfully and wonderfully made; not born into the world for sudden calamity or destruction, but an Original, made by G-O-D, unique and with a purpose.

Therefore, if anyone is in Christ, he is a new creation; old things have passed away; behold, all things have become new. 18 Now all things are of God, who has reconciled us to Himself through Jesus Christ, and has given us the ministry of reconciliation, 19 that is, that God was in Christ reconciling the world to Himself, not imputing their trespasses to them, and has committed to us the word of reconciliation. 20 Now then, we are ambassadors for Christ, as though God were pleading through us: we implore you on Christ's behalf, be reconciled to God. 21 For He made Him who knew no sin to be sin for us, that we might become the righteousness of God in Him.

II Corinthians 5:17-21

I am fearfully and wonderfully made – I am a person of faith.

Now faith is the substance of things hoped for, the evidence of things not seen. 2 For by it the elders obtained a good testimony. 3 By faith we understand that the worlds were framed by the word of God, so that the things which are seen were not made of things which are visible. 4 By faith Abel offered to God a more excellent sacrifice than Cain, through which he obtained witness that he was righteous, God testifying of his gifts; and through it he being dead still speaks. 5 By faith Enoch was taken away so that he did not see death, "and was not found, because God had taken him"; for before he was taken he had this testimony, that he pleased God. 6 But without faith it is impossible to please Him, for he who comes to God must believe that He is, and that He is a rewarder of those who diligently seek Him.

Hebrews 11:1-6

I am fearfully and wonderfully made — I am a person of hope.

Therefore, having been justified by faith, we have peace with God through our Lord Jesus Christ, through whom also we have access by faith into this grace in which we stand, and rejoice in hope of the glory of God.

And not only that, but we also glory in tribulations, knowing that tribulation produces perseverance; and pperseverance, character; and character, hope. Now hope does not disappoint, because the love of God has been poured out in our hearts by the Holy Spirit who was given to us.

Romans 5:1-5

I am fearfully and wonderfully made — I am a person of reverence for the Most High God.

LORD, our Lord, How excellent is Your name in all the earth, Who have set Your glory above the heavens! 2 Out of the mouth of babes and nursing infants You have ordained strength, Because of Your enemies, That You may silence the enemy and the avenger.

Psalms 8:1-2

I am fearfully and wonderfully made – I am a person of worship of the Most High God.

Oh come, let us worship and bow down; Let us kneel before the LORD our Maker.

Psalm 95:6

I am fearfully and wonderfully made – I am a person of prayer to the Most High God.

If My people who are called by My name will humble themselves, and pray and seek My face, and turn from their wicked ways, then I will hear from heaven, and will forgive their sin and heal their land.

II Chronicles 7:14

I am fearfully and wonderfully made!

TOUGH LOVE ON PAPER (TLOP)

LESSON 6

But be doers of the word, and not hearers only, deceiving yourselves. 23 For if anyone is a hearer of the word and not a doer, he is like a man observing his natural face in a mirror; 24 for he observes himself, goes away, and immediately forgets what kind of man he was. 25 But he who looks into the perfect law of liberty and continues in it, and is not a forgetful hearer but a doer of the work, this one will be blessed in what he does.

James 1:22-25

YES = Your Esteem Statement. What are your thoughts concerning your self-esteem, self-worth, and purpose?

For as he thinks in his heart, so is he.

Proverbs 23:7a

To help you formulate your statement, each lesson focuses on a truth from the Word of God that we will utilize as a self-esteem builder. Today's self-esteem builder: The truth that I know, that I understand, and that I apply that makes me free.

Then Jesus said to those Jews who believed Him, "If you abide in My word, you are My disciples indeed. 32 And you shall know the truth, and the truth shall make you free."

John 8:31-32

But Christ came as High Priest of the good things to come, with the greater and more perfect tabernacle not made with hands, that is, not of this creation. 12 Not with the blood of goats and calves, but with His own blood He entered the Most Holy Place once for all, having obtained eternal redemption. 13 For if the blood of bulls and goats and the ashes of a heifer, sprinkling the unclean, sanctifies for the purifying of the flesh, 14 how much more shall the blood of Christ, who through the eternal Spirit offered Himself without spot to God, cleanse your conscience from dead works to serve the living God?

Hebrews 9:12-14

The Blood of Jesus has purified or purged the conscience mind (the belief system) and Believers are set free from the bondage of past errors and mistakes. The Blood of Jesus does four (4) things:

- o Purifies or Purges,
- o Pardons,
- o Protects, and
- o Provides.

> So Satan answered the LORD and said, "Does Job fear God for nothing? 10 Have You not made a hedge around him, around his household, and around all that he has on every side? You have blessed the work of his hands, and his possessions have increased in the land.
>
> Job 1:9-10

The application of the Blood of Jesus is done with the words of your mouth: "Father, in the Name of Jesus, the Blood of Jesus is my purification, my pardon, my protection, and my provision. I plead the Blood of Jesus over me, my household, and my possessions. Thank you Father for the Blood of Jesus."

> I beseech you therefore, brethren, by the mercies of God, that you present your bodies a living sacrifice, holy, acceptable to God, which is your reasonable service. 2 And do not be conformed to this world, but be transformed by the renewing of your mind, that you may prove what is that good and acceptable and perfect will of God.
>
> Romans 12:1-2

Renew the mind with the Word of God on a daily basis so that every time the enemy attacks on purpose, you respond on purpose.

Attack on God's Word = Counter-attack with Numbers 23:19

> God is not a man, that He should lie, Nor a son of man, that He should repent. Has He said, and will

He not do? Or has He spoken, and will He not make it good?

Numbers 23:19

Attack on Your Worth = Counter-attack with I John 4:4.

You are of God, little children, and have overcome them, because He who is in you is greater than he who is in the world.

I John 4:4

Attack on Your Wisdom = Counter-attack with I Corinthians 1:30.

But of Him you are in Christ Jesus, who became for us wisdom from God — and righteousness and sanctification and redemption

I Corinthians 1:30

TOUGH LOVE ON PAPER (TLOP)

LESSON 7

But be doers of the word, and not hearers only, deceiving yourselves. 23 For if anyone is a hearer of the word and not a doer, he is like a man observing his natural face in a mirror; 24 for he observes himself, goes away, and immediately forgets what kind of man he was. 25 But he who looks into the perfect law of liberty and continues in it, and is not a forgetful hearer but a doer of the work, this one will be blessed in what he does.

James 1:22-25

YES = Your Esteem Statement.   What are your thoughts concerning your self-esteem, self-worth, and purpose?

For as he thinks in his heart, so is he.

Proverbs 23:7a

To help you formulate your statement, each lesson will focus on a truth from the Word of God that we will utilize as a self-esteem builder. Today's self-esteem builder: The truth that I know, that I understand, and that I apply is the truth that nobody can take away from me.

"Therefore hear the parable of the sower: 19 When anyone hears the word of the kingdom, and does not understand it, then the wicked one comes and snatches away what was sown in his heart. This is he who received seed by the wayside. 20 But he who received the seed on stony places, this is he who hears the word and immediately receives it with joy; 21 yet he has no root in himself, but endures only for a while. For when tribulation or persecution arises because of the word, immediately he stumbles. 22 Now he who received seed among the thorns is he who hears the word, and the cares of this world and the deceitfulness of riches choke the word, and he becomes unfruitful. 23 But he who received seed on the good ground is he who hears the word and understands it, who indeed bears fruit and produces: some a hundredfold, some sixty, some thirty."

Matthew 13:18-23

Keep the enemy from snatching the truth away from you by staying out of fear. Fear is a spirit, but not from God.

For God has not given us a spirit of fear, but of power and of love and of a sound mind.

II Timothy 1:7

The fear of failure will cause you to believe the lie that you must meet certain standards in order to feel good about yourself. The truth is God has justified you! It is just as if you'd never done it!

But God demonstrates His own love toward us, in that while we were still sinners, Christ died for us. 9 Much more then, having now been justified by His blood, we shall be saved from wrath through Him.

Romans 5:8-9

The fear of rejection will cause you to believe that you must be approved or accepted by certain others in order to feel good about myself. The truth is you are a child of God.

The Spirit Himself bears witness with our spirit that we are children of God,

Romans 8:16

The fear of punishment will cause you to play "The Blame Game;" blaming others for your failure; feeling unworthy of love, therefore deserving to be punished. The truth is you are forgiven. The sin debt is paid-in-full with the Blood of Jesus.

He has delivered us from the power of darkness and conveyed us into the kingdom of the Son of His love, 14 in whom we have redemption through His blood, the forgiveness of sins.

Colossians 1:13-14

Keep the enemy from snatching the truth away from you by staying out of shame, guilt, and condemnation.

The shame, guilt, and condemnation will cause you to play "The Shame Game;" fearing being uncovered or discovered, making cover-ups for your mess-ups, believing you are hopeless and cannot change. The truth is you are a new creature.

> Jesus answered and said to him, "Most assuredly, I say to you, unless one is born again, he cannot see the kingdom of God." 4 Nicodemus said to Him, "How can a man be born when he is old? Can he enter a second time into his mother's womb and be born?" 5 Jesus answered, "Most assuredly, I say to you, unless one is born of water and the Spirit, he cannot enter the kingdom of God. 6 That which is born of the flesh is flesh, and that which is born of the Spirit is spirit.
>
> John 3:3-6

TOUGH LOVE ON PAPER (TLOP)

LESSON 8

But be doers of the word, and not hearers only, deceiving yourselves. 23 For if anyone is a hearer of the word and not a doer, he is like a man observing his natural face in a mirror; 24 for he observes himself, goes away, and immediately forgets what kind of man he was. 25 But he who looks into the perfect law of liberty and continues in it, and is not a forgetful hearer but a doer of the work, this one will be blessed in what he does.

James 1:22-25

YES = Your Esteem Statement. What are your thoughts concerning your self-esteem, self-worth, and purpose?

For as he thinks in his heart, so is he.

Proverbs 23:7a

To help you formulate your statement, each lesson will focus on a truth from the Word of God that we will utilize as a self-esteem builder. Today's self-esteem builder: I can never rise above the image that I have of myself.

Then Moses sent them to spy out the land of Canaan, and said to them, "Go up this way into the South, and go up to the mountains, 18 and see what the land is like: whether the people who dwell in it are strong or weak, few or many; 19 whether the land they dwell in is good or bad; whether the cities they inhabit are like camps or strongholds; 20 whether the land is rich or poor; and whether there are forests there or not. Be of good courage. And bring some of the fruit of the land." Now the time was the season of the first ripe grapes. 25 And they returned from spying out the land after forty days. 26 Now they departed and came back to Moses and Aaron and all the congregation of the children of Israel in the Wilderness of Paran, at Kadesh; they brought back word to them and to all the congregation, and showed them the fruit of the land. 27 Then they told him, and said: "We went to the land where you sent us. It truly flows with milk and honey, and this is its fruit. 28 Nevertheless the people who dwell in the land are strong; the cities are fortified and very large; moreover we saw the descendants of Anak there. 29 The Amalekites dwell in the land of the South; the Hittites, the Jebusites, and the Amorites dwell in the mountains; and the Canaanites dwell by the sea and along the banks of the Jordan."

30 Then Caleb quieted the people before Moses, and said, "Let us go up at once and take possession, for we are well able to overcome it." 31 But the men who had gone up with him said, "We are not able to go up against the people, for they are stronger than we." 32 And they gave the children of Israel a bad report of the land which they had spied out, saying, "The land through which we have gone as

spies is a land that devours its inhabitants, and all the people whom we saw in it are men of great stature. 33 There we saw the giants (the descendants of Anak came from the giants); and we were like grasshoppers in our own sight, and so we were in their sight."

Numbers 13:17-20; 25-33

Here in Numbers chapter 13, notice the words "see", "sight", "saw." God told them "the land which I give." God already knew that they needed some evidence, some proof of what He had promised. They had the fruit, but that was apparently not enough. Twelve men went out to the land of Canaan, the Promised Land, but only two men were of faith, Joshua and Caleb. Ten men could not rise about the image of defeat. Israel wandered around in the wilderness for forty (40) years; time for those in rebellion, those who murmured against God, those who were in doubt and fear, to die off. So whatever happened to Joshua and Caleb?

Twelve spies were sent to see the land. Ten came back with a negative report and two came back with a positive report – Joshua and Caleb were those two young men.

Caleb was the one to still the people when they got excited about the giants in the land.

When Israel rebelled and angered God, it was Joshua and Caleb who begged the people to trust God.

Joshua and Caleb were rewarded with entering the promise land.

Moses died and Joshua became the new leader.

Then the word of the LORD came to me, saying: 5 "Before I formed you in the womb I knew you; Before you were born I sanctified you; I ordained you a prophet to the nations." 6 Then said I: "Ah, Lord GOD! Behold, I cannot speak, for I am a youth." 7 But the LORD said to me: "Do not say, 'I am a youth,' For you shall go to all to whom I send you, And whatever I command you, you shall speak. 8 Do not be afraid of their faces, For I am with you to deliver you," says the LORD.

Jeremiah 1:4-8

Are you beginning to see yourself?

TOUGH LOVE ON PAPER (TLOP)

LESSON 9

But be doers of the word, and not hearers only, deceiving yourselves. 23 For if anyone is a hearer of the word and not a doer, he is like a man observing his natural face in a mirror; 24 for he observes himself, goes away, and immediately forgets what kind of man he was. 25 But he who looks into the perfect law of liberty and continues in it, and is not a forgetful hearer but a doer of the work, this one will be blessed in what he does.

James 1:22-25

YES = Your Esteem Statement. What are your thoughts concerning your self-esteem, self-worth, and purpose?

For as he thinks in his heart, so is he.

Proverbs 23:7a

To help you formulate your statement, each lesson will focus on a truth from the Word of God that we will utilize as a self-esteem builder. Today's self-esteem builder: God's Word protects and preserves our identity, our value, our worth, and our potential.

Then the king instructed Ashpenaz, the master of his eunuchs, to bring some of the children of Israel and some of the king's descendants and some of the nobles, 4 young men in whom there was no blemish, but good-looking, gifted in all wisdom, possessing knowledge and quick to understand, who had ability to serve in the king's palace, and whom they might teach the language and literature of the Chaldeans. 5 And the king appointed for them a daily provision of the king's delicacies and of the wine which he drank, and three years of training for them, so that at the end of that time they might serve before the king. 6 Now from among those of the sons of Judah were Daniel, Hananiah, Mishael, and Azariah. 7 To them the chief of the eunuchs gave names: he gave Daniel the name Belteshazzar; to Hananiah, Shadrach; to Mishael, Meshach; and to Azariah, Abed-Nego.

8 But Daniel purposed in his heart that he would not defile himself with the portion of the king's delicacies, nor with the wine which he drank; therefore he requested of the chief of the eunuchs that he might not defile himself. 9 Now God had brought Daniel into the favor and goodwill of the chief of the eunuchs. 10 And the chief of the eunuchs said to Daniel, "I fear my lord the king, who has appointed your food and drink. For why should he see your faces looking worse than the young men who are your age? Then you would endanger my head before the king."

11 So Daniel said to the steward whom the chief of the eunuchs had set over Daniel, Hananiah, Mishael, and Azariah, 12 "Please test your servants for ten days, and let them give us vegetables to eat and

water to drink. 13 Then let our appearance be examined before you, and the appearance of the young men who eat the portion of the king's delicacies; and as you see fit, so deal with your servants." 14 So he consented with them in this matter, and tested them ten days.

15 And at the end of ten days their features appeared better and fatter in flesh than all the young men who ate the portion of the king's delicacies. 16 Thus the steward took away their portion of delicacies and the wine that they were to drink, and gave them vegetables. 17 As for these four young men, God gave them knowledge and skill in all literature and wisdom; and Daniel had understanding in all visions and dreams.

18 Now at the end of the days, when the king had said that they should be brought in, the chief of the eunuchs brought them in before Nebuchadnezzar. 19 Then the king interviewed them, and among them all none was found like Daniel, Hananiah, Mishael, and Azariah; therefore they served before the king. 20 And in all matters of wisdom and understanding about which the king examined them, he found them ten times better than all the magicians and astrologers who were in all his realm. 21 Thus Daniel continued until the first year of King Cyrus.

Daniel 1:3-21

Daniel and his friends (Shadrach, Meshach, and Abed-Nego) were in captivity and experienced favor with God and favor with men. They refused to compromise, but held fast to God, His Word, and His Ways.

> The king answered Daniel, and said, "Truly your God is the God of gods, the Lord of kings, and a revealer of secrets, since you could reveal this secret." 48 Then the king promoted Daniel and gave him many great gifts; and he made him ruler over the whole province of Babylon, and chief administrator over all the wise men of Babylon. 49 Also Daniel petitioned the king, and he set Shadrach, Meshach, and Abed-Nego over the affairs of the province of Babylon; but Daniel sat in the gate of the king.
>
> Daniel 2:47-49

Daniel interpreted the King's dream and received promotion. Daniel used his "favor" with the King to "bless" his friends.

When under attack in Daniel chapter 3 for refusing to bow down to the golden image or serve the idol gods, Shadrach, Meshach, and Abed-Nego were placed in a fiery furnace, that was heated seven times hotter, its flames killing the very men that cast them bound into the fire.

> Then King Nebuchadnezzar was astonished; and he rose in haste and spoke, saying to his counselors, "Did we not cast three men bound into the midst of the fire?" They answered and said to the king, "True, O king." 25 "Look!" he answered, "I see four men loose, walking in the midst of the fire; and they are not hurt, and the form of the fourth is like the

Son of God." 26 Then Nebuchadnezzar went near the mouth of the burning fiery furnace and spoke, saying, "Shadrach, Meshach, and Abed-Nego, servants of the Most High God, come out, and come here." Then Shadrach, Meshach, and Abed-Nego came from the midst of the fire. 27 And the satraps, administrators, governors, and the king's counselors gathered together, and they saw these men on whose bodies the fire had no power; the hair of their head was not singed nor were their garments affected, and the smell of fire was not on them. 28 Nebuchadnezzar spoke, saying, "Blessed be the God of Shadrach, Meshach, and Abed-Nego, who sent His Angel and delivered His servants who trusted in Him, and they have frustrated the king's word, and yielded their bodies, that they should not serve nor worship any god except their own God! 29 Therefore I make a decree that any people, nation, or language which speaks anything amiss against the God of Shadrach, Meshach, and Abed-Nego shall be cut in pieces, and their houses shall be made an ash heap; because there is no other God who can deliver like this." 30 Then the king promoted Shadrach, Meshach, and Abed-Nego in the province of Babylon.

Daniel 3:24-30

GOD'S WORD PROTECTS AND PRESERVES OUR IDENTITY, OUR VALUE, OUR WORTH, AND OUR POTENTIAL.

It is your responsibility to protect and maintain your purpose, your value, your self-worth. Your Esteem Statement (YES) will come to pass through:

- Investment – It will cost you something

- Appreciation – It must become valuable to you

- Maintenance – It will require upkeep to sustain its efficiency

Failure to do your part could result in:

- Corruption – It will erode or die if proper care is not given

GOD'S WORD PROTECTS AND PRESERVES OUR IDENTITY, OUR VALUE, OUR WORTH, AND OUR POTENTIAL.

TOUGH LOVE ON PAPER (TLOP)

LESSON 10

There are many definitions for the word "confront", but relative to tough love, "to come face-to-face" is a good description of what should occur when we "confront." The objective of coming face-to-face is to address the misbehavior, to bring the person to a point of admission and repentance, and to agree on a plan of action for the future of the relationship.

ALL RELATIONSHIPS NEED GUIDELINES. Enforce the guidelines you have set in an effort to avoid the reoccurrence of the misbehavior. Below are examples of four (4) instructions and guidelines that are given to those who express a desire to overcome drug and alcohol addictions:

1. **Allow someone else (a person that has your best interest at heart) to handle your money.**

2. **Keep someone (a person that has your best interest at heart) with you at all times.**

3. **Be accountable for your time.**

4. **Attend a Bible-believing, Bible-teaching church on a regular basis.**

WHEN DO WE NEED TO COME FACE-TO-FACE?

When clear instructions and clear guidelines have been disobeyed or disregarded. God gave Adam clear instructions and clear guidelines.

> Then the Lord God took the man and put him in the Garden of Eden to tend and keep it. 16 And the LORD God commanded the man, saying, "Of every tree of the garden you may freely eat; 17 but of the tree of the knowledge of good and evil you shall not eat, for in the day that you eat of it you shall surely die."
>
> Genesis 2:15-17

GOD WAS CLEAR. Mankind (male and female) was created to preserve and to stand guard over all God had entrusted into our hands, to fulfill divine purpose in the earth. **WE WERE TO BE AN EXPRESSION OF JESUS CHRIST.**

> Then God said, "Let Us make man in Our image, according to Our likeness; let them have dominion over the fish of the sea, over the birds of the air, and over the cattle, over all the earth and over every creeping thing that creeps on the earth."
>
> Genesis 1:26

REPRESENTATION OF GOD

So God created man in His own image; in the image of God He created him; male and female He created them. 28 Then God blessed them, and God said to them, "Be fruitful and multiply; fill the earth and subdue it; have dominion over the fish of the sea, over the birds of the air, and over every living thing that moves on the earth."

Genesis 1:27-28

CARE OF THE THINGS OF GOD

Out of the ground the LORD God formed every beast of the field and every bird of the air, and brought them to Adam to see what he would call them. And whatever Adam called each living creature, that was its name. 20 So Adam gave names to all cattle, to the birds of the air, and to every beast of the field. But for Adam there was not found a helper comparable to him.

Genesis 2:19-20

FELLOWSHIP WITH GOD

And they heard the sound of the Lord God walking in the garden in the cool of the day, and Adam and his wife hid themselves from the presence of the Lord God among the trees of the garden.

Genesis 3:8

God was clear. Provision was made for Adam's natural and spiritual needs:

- For the Body – The Garden was designed to meet his physical needs

- For the Soul - Eve was created to be his companion, help-mate, fit and adaptable to him

- For the Spirit – The Tree of the knowledge of good and evil was designed to help him learn obedience. Spiritual maturity would come as a direct result of spiritual obedience.

With purpose defined and provision made, all Adam had to do was obey God. Adam chose to disobey.

> And Adam was not deceived, but the woman being deceived, fell into transgression.
>
> I Timothy 2:14

Adam even attempted to cover-up his mess-up.

> So when the woman saw that the tree was good for food, that it was pleasant to the eyes, and a tree desirable to make one wise, she took of its fruit and ate. She also gave to her husband with her, and he ate. 7 Then the eyes of both of them were opened, and they knew that they were naked; and they sewed fig leaves together and made themselves coverings.
>
> Genesis 3:6-7

GOD WAS CLEAR.

> Then the LORD God called to Adam and said to him, "Where are you?"
>
> Genesis 3:9

Now God is omnipotent (all-powerful). God is omnipresent (all-present). God is omniscient (all-knowing). God knows your location. The question is asked, not to inform God, but to help you locate yourself. "Do you know where you are?"

We have already identified "the who" and determined the "where." The next question is the "what."

> And the LORD God said to the woman, "What is this you have done?"
>
> Genesis 3:13

There is a difference between the person (the "who") and their performance (the "what). Address the performance. Avoid attacking the person. Significant Others, you are not the blame, so keep your cool. Remember, a soft word turns away wrath, but grievous words stir up anger (Proverbs 15:1) Screaming, yelling, ranting and raving won't make them see.

THEY CAN'T SEE BECAUSE THEY ARE SPIRITUALLY BLIND.

Whose minds the god of this age has blinded, who do not believe, lest the light of the gospel of the glory of Christ, who is the image of God, should shine on them.

II Corinthians 4:4

When clear instructions and clear guidelines have been disobeyed or disregarded and the misbehaving person is truly repentant (like the prodigal son in Luke 15:18 – "I have sinned,") be appreciative of the confession, and be prepared to implement the clear consequences and clear penalties.

TOUGH LOVE ON PAPER (TLOP)

LESSON 11

All misbehavior should be rewarded with consequences. Consequences are defined (for the purpose of this book) as the penalties imposed for a person's misbehavior. As a Significant Other, you are not the blame, but you have a responsibility (the ability to respond) to have a response plan ready to address the misbehavior.

When clear instructions and clear guidelines have been disobeyed or disregarded, then clear consequences and clear penalties have to be implemented. Notice the actions that God took in the next Scripture.

> So He drove out the man; and He placed cherubim at the east of the garden of Eden, and a flaming sword which turned every way, to guard the way to the tree of life.

> Genesis 3:24

God responded to this disobedience encounter and in spite of their attempts to blame one another, no participant escaped the consequences:

- The Serpent

  Crawl on his belly and eat dust, enmity between his seed and the woman's seed, his head bruised by Jesus Christ (the seed of the woman) and he would bruise the heel of Jesus Christ.

- The Woman

  Sorrow in conception, pain in childbirth, longing for her husband who would rule over her.

- The Man

  Struggle to make a living from the ground, sweat while your work the ground, and when you die - return to the ground.

When clear instructions and clear guidelines have been disobeyed or disregarded, then clear consequences and clear penalties have to be implemented. The misbehaving person must be allowed to experience the pain of their decisions. Many times, that pain is a motivation for change. The pain gets their attention and will not subside until something is done to relieve it.

Significant Others, "Don't get in the way of the pain!" Yes, it could mean that the:

1. Misbehaving employee – may experience loss of employment

2. Misbehaving child – may experience loss of privileges

3. Lawbreaker – may experience loss of freedom

4. Substance abuser – may experience loss of family and friends

Restrain your emotions. Resist the temptation to rescue. Maintain your tough love stand. It's temporary pain; keep your eyes on the permanent gain.

"DON'T GET IN THE WAY OF THE PAIN!"

The ultimate goal is to bring the misbehaving person to a point of decision. Present them with options like:

- "Your response can be to accept the consequences of your misbehavior and change, or

- "Your response can be to rebel and counterattack."

- "Whatever your response, I am prepared to follow-through with my response." (You need to be prepared to do whatever you said you would do.)

Throughout the process of implementing consequences, continue to give loving intervention by:

1. Reassuring the person of God's love

2. Reassuring the person of your love and also

3. Reassuring the person that you will not continue "as

is" if they refuse to change

If the decision is made not to accept the consequences of misbehavior and the person is unwilling to change, be prepared with your response before the confrontation. Rehearse what you plan to say; write it down if necessary.

If the decision is made to accept the consequences of misbehavior and change, it is a significant step in the right direction toward repentance. The word "repent" means to change the mind or purpose; to regret or to be sorrowful; to turn away from and return back to.

> If we confess our sins, He is faithful and just to forgive us our sins and to cleanse us from all unrighteousness.
>
> I John 1:9

For even if I made you sorry with my letter, I do not regret it; though I did regret it. For I perceive that the same epistle made you sorry, though only for a while. 9 Now I rejoice, not that you were made sorry, but that your sorrow led to repentance. For you were made sorry in a godly manner, that you might suffer loss from us in nothing. 10 For godly sorrow produces repentance leading to salvation, not to be regretted; but the sorrow of the world produces death. 11 For observe this very thing, that you sorrowed in a godly manner: What diligence it produced in you, what clearing of yourselves, what indignation, what fear, what vehement desire, what zeal, what vindication! In all things you proved yourselves to be clear in this matter.

II Corinthians 7:8-12 8

There are two types of repentance mentioned in this passage:

1. GODLY SORRY

You take actions or produce works over a period of time that clearly prove to God and others that you regret the offenses committed against them (whatever you have done) and you work to prove yourself clear of the matter.

This form of repentance works to life.

Therefore bear fruits worthy of repentance.

Matthew 3:8

2. WORLDLY SORRY

Not Godly sorry. You are just sorry you got caught! Your repentance is just for a season, just long enough to deceive the other person into trusting you again. No proving; no clearing of the matter.

This form of repentance works to death.

Let no one say when he is tempted, "I am tempted by God"; for God cannot be tempted by evil, nor does He Himself tempt anyone. 14 But each one is tempted when he is drawn away by his own desires and enticed. 15 Then, when desire has conceived, it gives birth to sin; and sin, when it is full-grown, brings forth death.

James 1:13-15

King David had committed adultery and murder. God was displeased with David's ungodly actions and sent the Prophet Nathan to implement the consequences. David repented, God forgave him, but the clear consequences/clear penalties were not revoked. The first child born to David and Bathsheba died.

King David cried out to God in Psalm 51:1 - "Have mercy upon me, O God, according to Your loving-kindness; according to the multitude of Your tender mercies, Blot out my transgressions." The God of mercy answered and enabled King David to overcome the consequences of his sins. God blessed David and Bathsheba with a second son, Solomon.

On that night God appeared to Solomon, and said to him, "Ask! What shall I give you?" 8 And Solomon said to God: "You have shown great mercy to David my father, and have made me king in his place. 9 Now, O LORD God, let Your promise to David my father be established, for You have made me king over a people like the dust of the earth in multitude. 10 Now give me wisdom and knowledge, that I may go out and come in before this people; for who can judge this great people of Yours?" 11 Then God said to Solomon: "Because this was in your heart, and you have not asked riches or wealth or honor or the life of your enemies, nor have you asked long life—but have asked wisdom and knowledge for yourself, that you may judge My people over whom I have made you king— 12 wisdom and knowledge are granted to you; and I will give you riches and wealth and honor, such as none of the kings have had who were before you, nor shall any after you have the like."

II Chronicles 1:7-12

"DON'T GET IN THE WAY OF THE PAIN!"

TOUGH LOVE ON PAPER (TLOP)

LESSON 12

When clear instructions and clear guidelines have been disobeyed or disregarded, then clear consequences and clear penalties have to be implemented in order for there to be a clear plan for restoration and clear reconciliation.

God provided the biblical model for tough love when He demonstrated his unconditional love for mankind:

1. He gave clear instructions and clear guidelines – God put the man in the Garden

2. He implemented clear consequences and clear penalties: God drove the man out of the Garden

3. He provided a clear plan for restoration and clear reconciliation - God gave the man the plan.

THE PLAN:

Therefore, just as through one man sin entered the world, and death through sin, and thus death spread to all men, because all sinned—

Romans 5:12

For all have sinned and fall short of the glory of God,

Romans 3:23

All have sinned, not "ya'll" have sinned. We were born sinners, but no problem; just get born-again!

THIS IS THE NEED!

For God so loved the world that He gave His only begotten Son, that whoever believes in Him should not perish but have everlasting life.

John 3:16

For by grace you have been saved through faith, and that not of yourselves; it is the gift of God, 9 not of works, lest anyone should boast.

Ephesians 2:8-9

God's love **brought** us back!

And God's love **bought** us back!

THIS IS THE SOLUTION!

But as many as received Him, to them He gave the right to become children of God, to those who believe in His name:

John 1:12

Believers have the covenant right, the privilege to be called the "Sons of God."

THIS IS THE REWARD!

That if you confess with your mouth the Lord Jesus and believe in your heart that God has raised Him from the dead, you will be saved. 10 For with the heart one believes unto righteousness, and with the mouth confession is made unto salvation. 11 For the Scripture says, "Whoever believes on Him will not be put to shame."12 For there is no distinction between Jew and Greek, for the same Lord over all is rich to all who call upon Him. 13 For "whoever calls on the name of the Lord shall be saved."

Romans 10:9-13

THIS IS THE REQUIREMENT!

God provided a clear plan for restoration and clear reconciliation by confessing with our mouth the Lord Jesus and believing in our heart that God raised Jesus from the dead, we are saved.

Everything that Adam messed-up with his disobedience in the Garden, Jesus Christ cleaned-up with his Blood on the Cross. If you want to receive Jesus Christ as your personal

Lord and Savior, then repeat this prayer:

Dear God,

I know without Jesus I am lost.

I believe your Word according to Romans 10:9-10 That if I confess with my mouth the Lord Jesus and believe in my heart that God raised Jesus from the dead, That I shall be saved. Jesus, I invite you into my life and receive you by faith as my Savior and my Lord. Satan, you don't have me anymore. I belong to Jesus and from this day forward, Him only will I serve. I repent of all my sins. Thank you for your forgiveness. Thank you, Father for saving me.

In Jesus' name.

Amen

THE PLAN BENEFITS

(A High-level Summary from Psalms 103:1-6)

1 Bless the LORD, O my soul;

And all that is within me, bless His holy name!

2 Bless the LORD, O my soul,

And forget not all His benefits:

3 Who forgives all your iniquities,

Who heals all your diseases,

4 Who redeems your life from destruction,

Who crowns you with loving-kindness and tender mercies,

5 Who satisfies your mouth with good things,

So that your youth is renewed like the eagle's.

6 The LORD executes righteousness

And justice for all who are oppressed.

TOUGH LOVE ON PAPER (TLOP)

LESSON 13

OPTIONS FOR HELP
THE FIRM

13223 Aldine Westfield Road

Houston, Texas 77039

Phone: (281) 449-5996

Fax: (281) 586-0317

www.TheFirmRecovery.org

SERVICES & PROGRAMS OFFERED

FAMILIES IN RECOVERY MATTER –
"FIRM Matters"
Thursdays – 7:30 pm

*Family development & healing for family members &
significant others*

Families In Recovery Matter is a support group based on a series of classes for spouses, adult family members and significant others who have loved ones in recovery. These classes focus on demonstrating what a healthy adult support system looks like for those with loved ones in recovery from drugs, alcohol, sexual addictions, or any form of addictive behavior.

THE CHILD OF RECOVERY EQUALLY MATTERS! –
"C.O.R.E. MATTERS!" Youth Development Program
Thursdays – 7:30 pm

Youth development & healing for children and teens with addictive parents

Studies show that having a parent in recovery from addiction and/or imprisonment is devastating on a child. Focusing entirely on the adult in recovery, the *Child Of Recovery* often gets left out. This program provides the healing environment, life skills, support systems, and services needed for children of addictive parents participating in the F.I.R.M. Services include, but are not limited to:

- Safe and consistent childcare during recovery services
- Mental health counseling & supportive services
- Mentoring & recreational therapy
- Educational improvement & academic support
- Physical & spiritual youth development

FREEDOM INSTITUTE FOR RECOVERY MANAGEMENT – *"The Home"*
Transitional & 90-day residential housing for men in recovery management
24 hours/7 days per week

90-day transitional living center for the men in families recovering from substance abuse and addiction. The home focuses men on building a firm foundation for recovery and reentry into their families and society. Men spend a minimum of 90 days practicing three essential principles: foundation, framing, & finishing. These essentials are repeated for a lifetime of successful building with God, themselves, family, and society.

INDIVIDUAL AFTERCARE MATTERS - *"I AM Aftercare"*
Aftercare Support group and relapse prevention tools
Thursdays – 7:30 pm

For the rest of their lives individuals in recovery must continue to practice the same steps that led them to freedom. Aftercare at the F.I.R.M. consists of developing the individual spiritually and physically in areas of personal identity. "I AM Aftercare" offers year-round weekly gatherings providing lifetime identity principles that affirm, encourage, and empower individuals everyday.

FINANCIAL INTERVENTION & RELAPSE ECONOMICS –
"FIRE Prevention" - Economic recovery practices &
intervention
Thursdays – 7:30 pm

Research shows recovering addicts who participate in financial intervention increase their ability to stay free from gambling and addictive behaviors long term. The FIRM's FIRE Prevention series is an economic recovery system designed to minimize the monetary nightmares associated with addiction and relapse. The system works with the individual's employer and family using intervention methods to help those desiring to **stay free financially**.

The result?
- Reduced individual unemployment;
- Increased individual self-sufficiency;
- Decreased individual relapse and recidivism rates.

ABOUT THE AUTHOR

Pastor Brenda Stewart has a tremendous passion for God's word coupled with a love for God's people. She has a highly-contagious spirit of excellence that flows through every facet of her ministry. Having received her mandate from God, she obediently fulfills her calling as Pastor of Grace Restoration Church, Houston, Texas.

Called to the ministry in 1989, Sister Brenda began her ministry as an Addiction Recovery Minister, and Bible Teacher. In 2000, she and her husband, Founding Pastor Mitchell B. Stewart, Sr. were called to the pastorate and founded Grace Restoration Church, a historical haven for families and individuals seeking victory from substance abuse and all manner of addiction.

In 2010, the church gave birth to an additional organization, The Freedom Institute for Recovery Management (The FIRM), a name that fully characterizes the mandate and call of God on Pastor Mitchell and Pastor Brenda's lives as well as the spirit of the congregation. Pastor Brenda has seen the fulfillment of Galatians 6:1-10 in her life – *"Brethren, if a man be overtaken in a fault, ye which are spiritual, restore such a one in the spirit of meekness; considering thyself, lest thou also be tempted. 2 Bear ye one another's burdens, and so fulfill the law of Christ. 3 For if a man think himself to be something, when he is nothing, he deceiveth himself. 4 But let every man prove his own work, and then shall he have rejoicing in himself alone, and not in another. 5 For every man shall bear his own burden. 6 Let him that is taught in the word communicate unto him that teacheth in all good things. 7 Be not deceived; God is not mocked: for whatsoever a man soweth, that shall he also reap. 8 For he that soweth to his flesh shall of the flesh reap corruption; but he that soweth to the Spirit shall of the Spirit reap life everlasting. 9 And let us not be weary in well doing: for in due season we shall reap, if we faint not. 10 As we have therefore opportunity, let us do good unto all men, especially unto them who are of the household of faith."* (KJV)

In July 2013, she was ordained as Pastor by Dr. Apostle Mario Villela (Founder/President) and Dr. Pastor Regina Villela (Co-Founder/Vice President) of Servants of the Streets Family Worship & Training Center. In services each Sunday, the anointed leadership team of Pastor Mitchell and Pastor Brenda minister to the needs of the Grace Restoration Church congregation. With active ministries, Grace Restoration is making a difference in the lives of its people and the community. Pastor Brenda and Pastor Mitchell B. Stewart, Sr. are an anointed duo that God is using to make critical positive impacts in the lives of people.

Their vision is uncompromisingly clear with three central principles:

1. **The restoration of the unsaved** – There are men, women, boys and girls who have not received Jesus as their personal Savior and Lord according to Romans 10:9-10 which simply says to confess with our mouth the Lord Jesus Christ and believe in our hearts that God raised Jesus from the dead and we shall be saved.

2. **The restoration of the saved** – There are men, women, boys and girls who have been wounded, bruised, discouraged and are broken-hearted within the Body of Christ. They have had what we call a "bad church experience." Many are sitting on the sidelines and God wants us to bring them back to the forefront. We must help to bring the care, the concern, and the compassion of Jesus back into the Body of Christ.

3. **The restoration of the addicted** – There are men, women, boys and girls who are bound by all manner of drug and alcohol addiction. God wants to do the same thing in their lives as he did in the life of Pastor Brenda, who won the vigilant fight for her husband, Mitchell B. Sr., after he became addicted to crack-cocaine. The now Pastor Mitchell B. Stewart Sr. has been delivered and set free from addiction since March, 1992!

The Stewarts and the Grace Restoration Church family have secured a permanent church building location so that they can adequately meet the spiritual needs of their congregation. In addition, they have secured a free 90-day residence for men who express a desire to overcome drug and alcohol addiction – and they minister to the entire family and needs of the community each week! Praise God for the Vision!

Pastor Brenda has taken the gospel nationally across the United States. She has ministered in: Tennessee, Nebraska, Indiana, Illinois, Mississippi, as well as many local churches in and around Houston. In the secular marketplace, Pastor Brenda is known and respected as Brenda Stewart, an Administrative Professional. Her career journey commenced in 1977 as a Receptionist for Shelby County Hospital Authority and concluded in December, 2012 as an Executive Assistant to the North America Downstream Controller for Shell Oil Products USA.

Pastor Brenda is the founding leader of the Victorious Women of God Fellowship and hosts the Annual Women's Conference at Grace Restoration where over 200 females (adults and teenagers) are blessed each year with personal and spiritual refreshing. In addition, each week she serves her community by coaching and teaching the families of men recovering from drug, alcohol, and all manners of addiction along with her husband, Pastor Mitchell B. Stewart, Sr. at the Freedom Institute for Recovery Management (The FIRM) in Houston, Texas.

Sister Brenda has always been an excellent student. She graduated with honors in the top ten percent of her class at Central High School, Memphis, Tennessee where she received numerous academic awards. Brenda furthered her education at Shelby State Community College and on December 20, 1977, she married her high school sweetheart, Mitchell B. Stewart, Sr., the founding Pastor of Grace Restoration Church, Executive Pastor and Director of The Freedom Institute for Recovery Management. They are the proud parents of four: Mitchell, Jr., Swanesa, Brandon, and Alicia, all married and serving in ministry with their parents. Two sons-in-law: Nathaniel, Torrence and two daughters-in-law: Ashley, Lekeisha. Ten grandchildren: Viola, Diondre', Mitchell, III (Tre'), ZaCorey, Alijah, Aubrey, Isaiah, Britain, Ashtyn, and Torrence. As a dynamic ministry team, Pastor Brenda and Pastor Mitchell Sr. are dedicated servants of the Most High God, working together to make Grace Restoration Church and The FIRM a place where people are truly committed to "Restoring Lives by the Grace of God."

NOTES:

_____

_____

_____

_____

_____

_____

_____

_____

_____

_____

NOTES:

_____

_____

_____

_____

_____

_____

_____

_____

_____

_____

NOTES:

_____

_____

_____

_____

_____

_____

_____

_____

_____

NOTES:

_____

_____

_____

_____

_____

_____

_____

_____

_____

NOTES:

_____

_____

_____

_____

_____

_____

_____

_____

NOTES:

_____

_____

_____

_____

_____

_____

_____

_____

NOTES:

_____

_____

_____

_____

_____

_____

_____

_____

NOTES:

_____

_____

_____

_____

_____

_____

_____

_____

_____